My Decade in Hillbilly Hell

by

Mary A Stokes

DORRANCE PUBLISHING CO
EST. 1920
PITTSBURGH, PENNSYLVANIA 15238

Dorrance Publishing Co
585 Alpha Drive
Pittsburgh, PA 15238
Visit our website at *www.dorrancebookstore.com*

ISBN: 979-8-89211-064-8
eISBN: 979-8-89211-562-9

*I would like to dedicate this book to my three children:
Dillon. Austin and Sierra; without them I have nothing.*

Thank you to Dillon Wheat for the cover art!

PROLOGUE

I once believed that fate defined our destinies. Many things in our lives are out of our control and already pre-determined by this mantra. While some are what seem to be lucky or "in the right place" for good fortune; others are born under a dark cloud and just can't seem to get a break. I no longer agree with this perception.

Life is what we make it.

As I sit here and waves continue to crash upon the shore, and I feel the sand between my toes and the rushing of the water on my feet, and I am in awe of this spectacular body of water, I am constantly reminded of how infinite life is. I often come to the ocean in search of peace and clarity. The sun will be setting soon and the sight of it is a rare optical illusion. Just as the ebb and flow of the waves are constant but never the same; this sunset is an extraordinary event to witness and each one is distinctive and vibrant. It is life imitating art! I will never tire of this tradition.

You must believe that there is a higher power when you witness this phenomenon. The ocean and all its vastness are not manmade. The sun rises and sets; the moon does the same, and each day is a new day. All not manmade. Who is responsible for all of this? Each person has their own view; whether it be a great astronomical explosion, a religious belief in which God created the earth and all its properties in just six days, or we all evolved from apes or some other kind of animal.

Life is a series of subsets. Each decade we are different people. We literally "live and learn." No decade is alike. Do you believe in fate, or do you believe that life, our lives individually, is a picture of our actions? We choose what and when to do things, so…our lives are just a replay of what we chose.

I personally believe in both. I once believed fate controlled our destinies. I was much younger then, at least three decades ago, but I did. I was young and carefree and full of ideas and aspirations. I have learned much more since that time. This is my story, which I will call a "tragic comedy" entitled *My Decade in Hillbilly Hell*.

Chapter 1

Going through a divorce is a devastating experience for everyone. If, however, you run into the "man of your dreams" while going through a divorce, turn and run as fast as you can! Listen to that voice in your head! You must suffer during the end of a marriage. You need time to grieve. Time to learn is essential to the process. Jumping right back on that horse is a terrible trip you don't want to make. Trust me.

I wasn't that old during my first divorce, but I wasn't a "spring chicken" either. I have always been somewhat of a loner. It didn't bother me at all to be single. I loved my freedom. In my life, I have known many more people that just cannot be alone. They must always have a partner. Very strange to me. I would see them with someone for years and one day visit, and they had a new partner overnight! That fast! It makes you wonder how?

Everyone has that little voice in their head. I don't mean that in a derogatory way. Intuition is what it's called. When common sense tells you that this is "too good to be true," IT IS! We are not immortals; we have intuition for a reason. That reason is protection! We all need to learn that going through the painful processes is how we heal and learn to make better decisions. We all must learn to listen to our inner voices well, or we will pay for years...

This is my story about having to pay repeatedly for bad decisions I made. A story about how your feelings will tell you what is right, and how you should pay attention! Intuition is not to be taken lightly. No one enjoys regrets. Regrets, though, are a healthy part of renewal. Regrets remind us of where we came from and what we are running away from ... NO MORE REGRETS!

Grief is, and always will be, a sad process. If you take the time to learn while going through it, you can benefit in the end. I never jumped from one partner to the next, and I am not judging anyone that does. I have always taken my time and grieved the breakup process. No matter if it took years. I think you learn a lot about yourself during those times. To me, it's a growing time.

I am still paying, but through the therapeutic process of writing this, I will survive and grow.

Chapter 2

I guess you could say I grew up sheltered. I grew up protected from the big bad, imperfect world. I had an idealistic philosophy of life. I believed life was fair…do unto others etc. While this is wonderful, usually reality kicks in during puberty. You start middle school, and you are exposed to all other kids from different socioeconomic backgrounds. You begin to learn what "real" life is all about.

I was raised in a normal middle-class home. By the time I was in sixth grade, my parents divorced. Remember, I said this was normal. It was a growing result of the Women's Liberation movement happening. Women were returning to the workforce and leaving the stay-at-home parent duties. My mother worked my entire childhood. My mother raised me, and I never was without anything I needed.

I moved out of my mom's early and began my life in the REAL world. In my early twenties, many of my friends were getting married and having babies. I was not ready for that. I was just enjoying my freedom of living on my own. Many days, Kraft mac and cheese was dinner. To this day, I still love those forbidden carbs! By my mid-twenties things changed. I began to yearn for a "family life" like so many of my friends had. My inner "time clock" was screaming at me, "It's now or never!"

That internal time clock of mine, I thought, was telling me that it was time to get married and settle down. Was it really, though? I took cues from all my friends at the time. Many were married and started families. I did want children but not necessarily marriage. At that time, though, you were frowned upon for even thinking about having a child out of wedlock. I guess I wanted marriage too.

My best friend at that time was Lulu. She was tall and slender, and always reminded me of a surfer girl. She talked in a very soft voice and was almost the opposite of me. She never had a problem with attracting the opposite sex. We spent most of our off time together. We both would go to the beach weekly and to various parties and never had a problem with being bored. There was plenty to do back then.

Lulu had gotten married, and it seemed like a blissful state. You really do need two people to raise a child or children. I spent most of my time working. I loved it. It's more than a job; it's about having daily co-workers to communicate with daily. It's a routine. You are never bored. You always have a place to go. Of course, the money you make is important too. Those bills just keep coming, and they don't pay themselves.

I did get married. It was not all it was cracked up to be though. When my first child was born, I was ecstatic! I loved being a mother. I quit my full-time job and stayed home with him. I enjoyed every minute. Watching him grow up, teaching him daily, and taking him to the library. Of course, Lulu had a baby too. She was only ten days older than my son.

We spent many days in her backyard suntanning and letting the kids swim in a little pool. Yes, I loved those times. After about two years of bliss, my husband wanted to move. We did. Being in a new city wasn't so nice for me. He had plenty of friends that he had grown up with, but I didn't. I missed my friends. Soon, though, I was pregnant with my second child. Another boy!

Chapter 3

When I married my first husband, I married for all the wrong reasons. I knew it then but felt it could not harm anything or anyone. I married a man who was six years younger than me. He had the looks, with that beautiful blond hair and blue eyes. We had a lot of good times together but in the end, he just was not meant to be married and faithful to one woman. He was quite the philanderer!

At the time, my best friend was Lulu... We both worked together and had our first children within a week apart and had even gotten married within a year of each other. We all spent time together weekly for barbecues and many social gatherings. Lulu and I had known each other during our teenage years and had rented apartments together. We were inseparable back then.

Eventually my husband wanted to move back to the city he was from so that we would be closer to his family. We did, and it was nice to have help from the grandparents. I missed Lulu, though, and all my friends, but Lulu and I spent hours a day on the phone comparing our children's progress and such. During this time, I had my second son. My husband sure made beautiful children! With two children, money was tight.

My husband came home one day and told me he could make great money if he went out of town to work. At first, I did not like the idea, but the money was good, and we needed it, so I agreed. One night as I awaited his arrival home from work, he came through the door with one red rose in his hand. I was wondering what the occasion was. As he hands the rose to me, he begins to tell me how every job he went to in the last year (since the job began) he had been unfaithful to me. He had met a new woman in every city! He felt better, he had BARED HIS SOUL to me! He said he felt much better! I was BLINDSIDED!

Needless to say we tried counseling. On the very first date with the marriage counselor, the therapist asked him what made him fall in love with me. He answered, "I loved her brown eyes!" The therapist almost spit her coffee out as she looked at me with my blue eyes! Six years together and he didn't even know what color my eyes were! We spoke to our pastor at the church as well but eventually we finally separated, and my two boys and I moved back home. Divorce was imminent! The only bright side in all of this was that I got to return to the city my friends and Lulu were in. At least I could cope better with familiar faces around.

Lulu was there when I arrived and her and her husband helped me move all the furniture into my new place. I loved it! The city we lived in was really popping back then! Plenty of stuff to do that was free! We all would go to what they called "Blues on the Green" on Wednesday nights. It was a huge park on the water and local up-and-coming musical bands would play. It was like a "hippie heaven." People would play frisbee and hacky sack and the kids could run around and play. It was as close to a "perfect paradise" as you could get.

Life back then was just different. We were all young and just starting on our journeys of life. When you are younger, you just have no idea what and where your life will take you. You live in the moment every day! No worries about tomorrow. You are loving just "getting by"! Eventually, life throws a few curveballs at you, and things must change. You learn that you must grow up! You will always have those memories, though. Pictures in your mind, if you will, that last a lifetime!

Just a couple of months after I returned, Lulu told me that she too was going to get a divorce! I was shocked!

The similarities in our lives were crazy! We both decided to take a trip to see her parents and my dad. Her father had gotten her a car and we would take the bus there and pick it up. On that day, an event would happen that would shake my world and turn it upside down. It would never be the same. You see, I was raised to believe that everyone is good, people are decent, and they all have a heart, don't they? Well... NO!

Divorce is not pretty. If there was no love to begin with, it wouldn't hurt so much. When children are involved, it is especially painful. Perhaps that is why there are so many pre-marriage workshops and counseling opportunities out there to take advantage of now. I remember when my mom told me, I was in sixth grade, that my father and her were getting a divorce. I was not upset at all. My father lived in our home but came home so late every day, I hardly saw him. They had never lived like they were "in love" like all my friends' parents did. They merely lived together in the same home but not together. I never saw any affection whatsoever.

I had a sister who was eight years older than me. She was killed, though, and she had just turned eighteen years old. I remember the day so clearly. I was riding my bike home from school and as I turned the last corner and was on my street, I saw my dad walking towards me. By then, I noticed my mom's car was in our driveway too. Neither one of them was ever home at that time. He held his arms out toward me and hugged me and told me, "Your sister Jackie has gone to heaven." I don't remember anything after that. I don't know if I cried or even clearly understood.

I was told that I would be staying at my friend's house for a few days. I was only ten then and didn't quite know how to grieve. I still cannot recall crying. I just don't remember. Meanwhile, a few doors down, at my house my parents were there alone, but with each other, grieving and planning her funeral. That was the day that ripped my family apart. It would never be the same.

Thinking back on it makes me sad now. My heart aches for my parents and the sadness they endured for the rest of their lives. Until I had children, I would never understand that most painful of all pains, losing a child. Having to go on raising another. I pray I never have to. If I do, I hope I can do it with as much grace, grit, and bravery as they did.

Had they had a strong foundation for their marriage, it might have survived. They both eloped when my mom was nineteen and moved south from Chicago, when they learned she was pregnant with my sister. That marital bliss did not last long. When I was born ten years later, I had never once seen it. In the 1950s in America, times were very different. You did not have a baby out of wedlock.

Chapter 4

Fate has a way with you. It rears its ugly head just when you least expect it. Well, Lulu and I were reunited again. We both were in the same city and we both were going through a divorce. Both of us, yet again, were facing a crisis in our lives at the same time. Strange how these things occur. Unexplainable but true.

Anyhow, here we were again in the city. The city where we both grew up. We had gone for the weekend. We both had separate lunch dates so we agreed we would meet back up at her parents' house after. I had lunch with my father. She had lunch with the Devil!

After lunch, my father dropped me off. He was there! Rex was there. I had been looking for him my whole life! He was my first crush, before I had even known what a crush was! His family had lived around the corner from my mom's house where I grew up. We played together as kids... We climbed trees, we rode bikes, and we got into mischief! I was a full-fledged tomboy and no matter how many times my dad scolded me for it, I loved playing with boys better!

I played hard and rough with all the boys and loved to get dirty. I had always wanted a brother and a bigger family. I flocked towards those families with lots of kids! Coming from a small family, it only made sense. Back then I played with Rex's sister Anissa, just so I could be around him! Daily I would ride my bike over to their house to play. One afternoon, though, was different. As I rode up their driveway, someone came out of the house to tell me that Rex and Anissa were not there. A terrible accident had occurred. Anissa and Rex had been playing with an uncle's rifle, and it had gone off. Anissa had been shot and she was in the hospital. Rex was downtown at the police station. Not soon after that, they had moved. I never saw them again. I never knew if Anissa lived or died. I was so sad. All I had were memories.

Over the years, I wondered what had happened to them. Did Anissa live? Where did they move? Time has a way of fading memories, but it never completely erases them. Throughout my teenage years and all my boyfriends, Rex remained in the back of my mind. I remember once in my teenage years, he rode by my house on a bicycle, and I just happened to be leaving at the time. We didn't talk that much that day, but I sure did want to. I guess no one ever forgets their first crush. As fate would have it, he came back into my life twenty-three years later.

Who remembers their first crush? They are a part of who we are. They are sweet memories from a child's perspective. A time before "life" took control of our lives. We were young, without a care in the world. Life hadn't taken over yet and changed our perspective of things. They were sweet memories that you hold onto but never forget. Most of us outgrow our first crush. Mine, though, was taken away by a tragedy. I never had the chance to outgrow it or move on. While I had many crushes in my childhood, the one that was snatched away so quickly would always remain in the back of my mind.

Throughout my teenage years, I experienced my first love, which is so dramatic, thinking back. That first love you think will last forever. You are inseparable from your love; you do everything together. You truly believe life could not get any better. One day something happens, and it is over. It really was not supposed to last forever, but instead, just a steppingstone on the way to your next love. Finally, in the process, you learn about what traits you admire in the opposite sex, and you begin to find out who you are and what you are looking for.

In my life, that is how it happened. I knew what I didn't want. I wanted what Hollywood portrayed as a "romantic" kind of love. A man that was full of confidence and would sweep me off my feet. A James Dean kind of rebellious "bad boy." They never are the marrying types, though, so while they are fun to dally with, they are not "keepers." I always thought true love would change them, but that is just a Hollywood folktale.

Chapter 5

As Lulu and I drove back home the conversation was all about Rex! I had no idea she knew him! She began to tell me about how she did. She told me Rex had been her first! I was astounded! How is it that her first and my first crush were the same guy? Until that day, neither one of us had ever mentioned him. What a peculiar incident!

Life can have some serious twists and turns in it. When stuff like this happens, your mind is in the middle of a whirlwind of confusion and amazement. It's hard to explain. Is this really reality or just a dream? Lulu and I had so many weird coincidences in our lives, I began to question it all. Is there some lesson I should be learning at this point or is it just another freak reality?

My mind was racing! I told her the story of my childhood with Rex. I wondered how I could know someone so well, and we both knew the same guy, but at different points in our lives. In retrospect, it seems Rex and his family moved to her neighborhood after the horrible accident. I didn't know her yet then. I learned too that Anissa, his sister, had survived the accident too. Life can be puzzling at times. Or was all this fate?

We continued the drive home in silence. I watched the beautiful valleys and trees as we passed them. I just couldn't keep my mind off

Rex though. I am sure Lulu was thinking too about Rex. Neither one of us brought the subject up again on that car ride. My two boys in her back seat sat quietly and napped along the way. I was ready to get home and relax.

Lulu dropped me off, and I went in to prepare dinner for the boys. The next day I went to work as usual and when I got home, I saw that Rex had called. What a surprise! He had said he was coming through town and needed a couch to sleep on. Could I help him out? Why sure! I called Lulu right away and told her! She told me he had called her too! Oh well, I thought, her loss is my gain! This was a red flag waving right in my face, but I'll be damned if I noticed it.

Chapter 6

The next day Rex showed up as planned! We stayed up half the night reliving old memories. I told him I was going through a divorce, and he was so sympathetic! He listened so intently and was so understanding. I marveled at how this could happen. The attraction to him was magnetic. He was unlike any other I had been with in my past. He really was not my type of guy, but his energy and his self-confidence were very appealing to me. He spoke of many things he had done in his life, and he seemed like a nomad to me, a world traveler. He also was so sweet. I had never met anyone like him.

As the days went by, he was still there. Helping with my boys and cooking. We became closer and one day he told me that he would like to stay and help me. In my eyes he was a "godsend!" I said, "Of course!" I enjoyed his company, and he was great with my kids, and I didn't have to do it all alone. I was rather immature back then, and anything that brought me instant gratification worked. I did not think about the ramifications or the future at all. I lived day to day.

As the days grew into months, we finally consummated the relationship. I was fully, head over heels in love with this man. I kept telling myself that since I was so heartbroken from the last relationship that God (or fate) had brought this man into my life, I had previously resolved to myself that I would be a single mom of two boys, and no man in his right mind wanted that. Most guys you meet wanted a single woman with no baggage. Yet, here was Rex! He wanted it! It was a miracle, I thought. How often, though, do miracles happen?

The courtship of this relationship was short and sweet. I fell head over heels for him. He began to open up about his past. He too had children. His exes had custody of them. Another red flag appeared! He told me he had previously had cancer and was unable to have any more children. Lastly, he explained he was running from the law. Wow!

Boom! He was a rebel, all right! Just what I thought I what looking for. Be careful what you wish for; you just might get it! At the time, I felt like the luckiest girl in the world. Here was this dark-headed mystery man that I knew very little about; still, I was intrigued. We got along great, had great times together, and he was so good with my two young sons.

It didn't matter in my immature mind what he said, I was in love with him. This man was helping me, and I was in love, I thought. Red flags or not, we would and could work together through all of this. He was perfect to me. Love, or infatuation, can sure blind you! I could not imagine my life without him. This poor man had been through hell and back and he needed my love and support.

He had helped me by swooping in and taking over my life. After my first marriage, I thought this was what I needed. Someone else was in control, and I loved it! He took the boys to McDonald's and picked them up from day care, and he was working too. I would get home from work and smell dinner cooking, and my boys would be safe and happy. Life was good. There was nothing that I feared or worried about.

About a month after, I learned I was pregnant. Another miracle! This time I was carrying a girl! He and I were excited, but it didn't last too long. One night as I walked in the door, I smelled the chicken-fried steak he was cooking! I walked in and greeted him. There he was, shirtless and shoeless, cooking dinner. I went to change and heard a knock at my door. I figured he would answer. When they knocked a second time, I went to answer. Lo and behold, it was the infamous Mr. Gadget, or so he was nicknamed. I had heard about him from Rex. He was the bounty hunter. He was dressed in a Dick Tracy hat just like I had been told. He had a buffed-up dude with him as a sidekick. He looked like a male stripper!

He asked about Rex, and I lied, of course, thinking Rex was still in my kitchen, finishing dinner. He asked if they could enter my apartment and I told him no. He began to spout off all of Rex's charges to me, as if that would make me change my mind. Suddenly, buff boy, his sidekick screams, "The back door is open. He must have gotten away!" I hadn't even noticed.

I closed the door and ran to the kitchen. All the food was done, and all the burners were turned off. Rex was indeed gone. He jumped over my patio gate and was on the run, still shoeless and shirtless in forty-degree weather! I was shocked! He called about an hour later, telling me he was on top of a liquor store, down the street, watching all the commotion, and he was cold.

He must have surrendered because I never heard from him again that night. They drove that ten-hour ride back and put him in jail. He had run for seven years, but he had slowed down with me for a few months, and now he was gone. For a long time, I was sure. I was heartbroken and pregnant!

Chapter 7

My mother even thought Rex was so charming! With all the trouble he was in, I just couldn't believe it. While he was gone, I wondered if I would ever see him again. If someone has been running for seven years and finally is captured, there is just no way they would be released, I thought. I had to just forget about him and move on with my messed-up life. It was a very sad moment in my life.

I called her that night and told her. Surprisingly, she was sympathetic. She had truly liked him. Her voice was always the voice of "practicality" to me. She was a realist! She immediately (she waited until the next day) went into "fix it" mode. She called the following day telling me she had researched, and there were many individuals, churches, and organizations out there who would either pay for an abortion or pay for the birth of the child and adopt it, once born. That is where my idealism trumped her realism. I could never give up my child! I would work as many jobs as it took. I would make this work! That is how my brain works. I would not even consider those notions!

His mother was apparently helping him though. Soon I learned that his mother and sister were not afraid to perjure themselves in court to help Rex. After about a week, he began calling me from jail. I told him I didn't know if I could keep the baby because I just couldn't afford it. My mom had mentioned adoption. Deep inside I knew I would keep this baby, because I carried her inside of me for so long. He begged me not to do anything rash, and just to take care of myself and the baby. He said soon he would be released, and he would be back. While I was relieved he had called, I really doubted he would get out. Obviously, I didn't know that much about the criminal justice system then.

He was only gone for a few weeks! He said the judge dropped the charges. I really didn't care. It was like a miracle. I couldn't believe it. I believed in fate, and that, I thought, was driving all these miracles. Everything about this whole situation was unbelievable to me. I was riding that wave of "excitement and joy" and excitedly anticipating the birth of my third child, a girl. We would have the perfect little family. I thanked God every night.

Just as he had said, within weeks he was back! He had said the judge let him out because he was dying of cancer! His mom and his sister confirmed that to the judge. Now as I look back, I know that was a lie! At the time, I didn't want to know the truth. I was ecstatic that the father of my baby was back! We both were happy. It really was one of the best times in my life.

He was out of jail and back in my life again! It was fate, right? My father had started becoming a regular visitor and I was forming a good relationship with him. He liked Rex too. My life felt whole now. My father had loved coming and playing with his two grandsons. I was still going through a divorce, but I was not grieving at all. It just didn't make sense to me. I just kept unapologetically riding that wave.

The next seven months before the birth went by quickly. My mom, Rex and I, and the boys moved into a nice house. It was gorgeous and had plenty of room for all of us. I worked a few blocks away and I would walk to work each day. It was a beautiful neighborhood and I enjoyed walking down the beautiful tree-lined streets and seeing all the birds and squirrels. It was good to exercise too. My life was a dream then.

Chapter 8

The day arrived for the scheduled birth, and we drove to the hospital. I worked that day. I got off at six P.M., and off to the hospital we went. Rex and I both were both filled with gleeful anticipation! I was induced, and the next day my daughter was born! Rex was there for all of it! His mom told me that our daughter was the first birth he had ever attended out of his children.

As the holidays approached, my newborn daughter was so tiny. Rex would hold her in one hand! She was small! My father came for Christmas that year and got to see her. He said she was beautiful. I am so glad he came and got to meet her. Little did I know it would be the last time my father would see her. The day went well, but as the festivities continued into the night, tragedy occurred.

It seems Rex had a violent streak in him when it came to drinking liquor. I had never seen it until then. Sadly, I wanted my father to help me, and he did not want to get involved. I was so hurt. The next day when he was leaving, he tried to hug me and say goodbye, but I was so mad and hurt I just walked away and said goodbye under my breath.

When you let pride get in the way of your feelings, you make stupid decisions which cause big mistakes and huge regret. My father knew Rex and I were fighting but he stayed out of it. All of us had been drinking heavily that night and it truly was a sad event. I am still ashamed of my behavior that day. I guess regret can last forever. I wanted my dad to save me from Rex's rage, and he didn't. I see now why he didn't... Now it is too late though.

My father left the next day. I know he was worried about me, and I felt horrible. My pride lasted one more day and I began calling him. I wanted to apologize for my stupid behavior. No answer, though. God only knows what his last thoughts of me and my life were.

Rex had given me the best apology he could and told me that he didn't need to drink alcohol. I agreed. He seemed very sad about the whole incident and even cried about it and then did what he could to convince me that it would never happen again. There were cracks in his armor I was beginning to see. How could a man that was so gentle and loving have so much rage? I did not like that side of him that showed that night, but the love I had for him was trying very hard to forget it. Wipe the slate clean. Red flags were blowing in the wind. When you are in love, you can justify anything, I guess.

Chapter 9

On New Year's Eve, my mom had gone out of town, and Rex and I were relaxing with the kids. The phone rang and I answered it. It was the coroner's office informing me that my father had died. I was devastated! He had just left less than a week ago. Did I cause this? The sadness I felt was indescribable.

I needed to go there and clean his apartment and plan for his funeral. I called my mom, asking for help; she told me I was on my own. What a shock! Now I would go plan a funeral! I soon learned that it would cost more to bury someone than to bring a child into the world! I was in a huge state of guilt-ridden shock!

That night we packed all the kids up and headed to the big city. Rex had family there so at least we had a place to stay. The next day the agent opened his apartment and let us in. As I began going through all his things, I was astounded by everything he had from me. The ceramic frog I had painted for him when I was in sixth grade! Awards I had won in my childhood were all there. Pictures, letters, everything! It was like looking back at my whole childhood! I was crying tears of joy!

Being in his apartment and realizing that he really had loved me and was proud of me was a very poignant point. I saw the ceramic frog that I made for him in sixth grade. I was so proud of that! There it was! He had kept all the things I made for him! Letters I had written to him from so long ago flooded my mind with happy memories! It was like walking through a time machine of my childhood! Sentimentality got to me, and I began to cry. Tears of joy!

When I was a teenager, I never thought he approved of me. He would say I was either too skinny or too fat. I tried and tried but nothing changed. I realize now that his father was like that too. His parents had been from up north and had believed in the "school of hard knocks." Not much affection was shown. As a child, seeing my friends' families acting differently, I always wanted that. Not in my family though. Although no affection was shown, there was love, and as I saw all the trinkets and such in his home that day, I realized this. It was a moment of clarity for me.

While I was reminiscing and amazed at this whole situation and still crying, Rex came in from another room with a bunch of papers in his hand. He had found a will! Granted this will was written on a bar napkin, but it was a will! I never believed my father had anything! He lived like a miser my whole life! It turns out he was left a substantial inheritance from his parents. He had invested it but never spent it! It was all for me! Or I should say, it should have been.

Chapter 10

After my father's funeral, Rex began a big push to move us to his hometown. It was in a different state! I objected at first, but I was so in love with him, I just couldn't see my life without him. He bragged about his family because, with me, there was just my mom! He had a big family and he kept saying that they would all help with the kids. My mom didn't babysit at all! If and when she did, she charged a fee.

Eventually I agreed. We set a date, and mid-summer we moved. I was so excited! We were supposed to buy a house with my inheritance but that didn't quite fit in with his plans. His sister, Anissa, lived there, and right next to her house was almost an acre of land. I bought that plot and a brand new double-wide trailer to put on it! It was huge and nice and shiny! I had never lived in a trailer before, so the sound the floor makes as people walk through, I figured I would learn to accept. I never did. I am adamantly against trailers now. Such a huge waste of money!

The ride there was long. Three kids and all our belongings crammed into a U-Haul. We were all excited to begin a new phase of our lives. The trailer I bought was the top of the line for that year. I couldn't imagine what it would be like on the land I bought. Even though I had my doubts about buying a trailer, I still was filled with hopeful emotions about this whole journey.

Gleeful anticipation is the best way to describe the emotions I felt. I had three beautiful children, I was so in love with a man I thought would be there for me and with me until the end, and I couldn't wait to meet this family of his that I had heard so much about! The drive there was long, and the whole way I pondered about how perfect my life, at that very moment, was. I couldn't think of a time when I felt so loved and happy.

We stopped halfway there and got to a motel. The kids needed a break, and after we heard "Are we there yet?" what seemed like a trillion times, we needed a break as well. We ate dinner and then took the kids for a swim in the pool. Then we all retired early. Long car rides are exhausting! I still found it hard to sleep because of the anticipation of this whole trip, but eventually I, too, nodded off.

The next morning, after a nice breakfast, we were on the road again. We arrived at our new home around five P.M. It was beautiful, for a trailer! The kitchen with the vaulted ceiling and huge open area was every woman's dream! I loved it! The kids had a huge backyard. The boys were running around with excitement. They each would have their own room. I was so happy!

We hadn't eaten since a snack for lunch, and I was getting hungry. Since we had no groceries, I suggested we order pizza to be delivered. His family looked at me with amusement. His family informed me that they don't have pizza delivery there! "What?" I asked myself. "What kind of place doesn't have pizza delivery?" And then, "What kind of town is this?" Well, let me tell you.

After being there a few short months, I realized this town was something like a decade or so behind, when it came to laws and such. People in this town could drive with an open container and it wasn't against the law! Nor did they need to wear seatbelts! And when I asked about recycling, everyone looked at me with shock! I was informed that we needed a "burn barrel," where you burned all your recycling! All I could think was, "What in the hell have I done?"

Where I grew up in a big city, you pulled your trash cans to the curb bi-weekly along with recycling. I didn't realize how convenient that was until I didn't have it. If you needed something from the corner store, it was just a hop, skip, or jump away. In this country town, there was nothing even remotely close to walk to, except a bar. I soon found out why I was never receiving my mail in a timely manner, because the postal delivery Jeep was always at the bar! Yes, the contrast between this town and the city I grew up in was black and white! Just to get to the nearest grocery store was a long ride! And those dark country roads were a nightmare to drive on at night!

What was in this town? His family was, and that was huge! After we got there, I began to meet them all! His mother was Maggie. She was impeccably dressed every time I saw her. Her fingers were always adorned with many gold and diamond rings. She was a tall, statuesque woman who never missed her weekly beauty shop appointment. Her hair was short and perfectly styled at all times. It was grey now but through pictures I learned it used to be black.

Rex, I learned, was the fifth child born to her out of six. She said they were all six born from her first husband, who had died of cancer years ago. She had them boy, girl, boy, girl, and boy, girl. When I met her, she had been married four more times after the death of her first and was single. She loved to gamble and complained constantly about being broke all the time. We got along for a while. There was so much more family to meet, though. She was just the tip of the iceberg!

I soon learned Rex had a cousin who was an integral part of his life. Her name was Layla Ann. She was a crackhead. Somehow, she had a magical power over him. She could call anytime of the day or night, and he would run to her aid. She was very thin and had blond hair. She had one daughter, who was Lila Ann. She, too, was a crackhead. Lila Ann, like her mother, was tall and skinny, with blondish-brown hair. They both were so skinny that it appeared they were malnourished to me. Her and her mom were more like "pimping pals," rather than mother and daughter. They both used their bodies, with men in and out of their family, for as long as I knew them. They were both in and out of jail the whole time I lived there. Apparently, that state didn't believe in habitual offenders.

Chapter 11

Where we moved was right next to his sister Anissa. All in the middle of nowhere! I soon learned that being the youngest of this whole family, Anissa was everyone's everything. She could have been a nurse in another life. She was a hypochondriac, though, so I guess that wouldn't have worked!

She was a big girl, over two hundred pounds, but she had a heart of gold. When she wasn't helping her mother Maggie, she would be Rex's "go-to" girl. She was a widow at a young age and lived in a house propped up on bricks adjacent to our property. Her husband had died of a heart attack while mowing the yard, just two weeks after being released from prison. He had been involved in a fatal DUI which had resulted in the death of a child. All of this happened just before we moved there. She had inherited the house on bricks.

She had a rich sugar daddy, though, and all the free medical that the government would provide, so she was fine. Reginald was her sugar daddy. He was an older man, retired veteran, and a normal guy with plenty of money. Why he got involved with this family, I will never know. It was the family's good fortune, I guess.

She was good with my children and didn't show partiality as all the rest of the family did regarding my two sons. She treated all children nicely and equally. I loved her then. She told me one time that I was such a good mom because I got up and cooked breakfast for my kids! *Doesn't every mom do that?* I thought. Well, no…I guess not?

We had been there for a few weeks, just trying to get water and septic installed. This was the county! Everyone in our area had wells on their land. I had never heard of such a thing. I soon learned about culverts and all the little nuances that were so different than in a big city, that were pertinent to have in this rural area we had moved to.

We had been there for about a week when I learned I could not put a well on my property. In this rural area there was no city water yet. Rex had called, and I had paid over a thousand dollars for a well, but two days later the septic tank people came. They informed me that they could not install one until I capped the well off.

The rules involving the required distance between a well and a septic tank could not be managed on my property. Also…Rex was never one to follow rules. It was pie shaped, and there just wasn't enough footage even though I had three quarters of an acre! Shocking. Well, I had to pay another nine hundred dollars to cap the well off and abandon the well and hope city water would be available soon. Anissa had a well next door; we would end up using hers for years. We had to have a septic tank though.

I finally figured out that Rex was supposed to install the septic tank first and then find a spot somewhere on the land after that to put the well. He did not. He just went off half-baked on everything. Why worry? He was not spending any money. I was. He sure could wastefully go through my money! Little did I know, this was just the beginning. Meanwhile, his mother and sister were always around. His mother was so proud of him.

Rex was not having a problem spending my inheritance in foolish ways, and it was beginning to bother me! There were more important things though at that very moment that we needed to think about, according to Maggie. According to her, we had to throw a housewarming party!

Chapter 12

A housewarming party sounded like a great idea! I would be able to meet more of this huge family. Secondly, it took my mind off Rex's spending habits with my inheritance! Anissa and I went to the grocery store and got a variety of foods for the occasion. We would have a fruit platter, a vegetable platter, and finger sandwiches. Maggie had given me over forty names and addresses, and all the invitations had been sent weeks before. I was excited!

What really bothered me was the distance we were from everything except one bar. Every time we needed something, we had to jump in the car and drive for what seemed like a million miles to me. Nothing was close! Why do people live so secluded like that? You get to know your neighbors, and there were no streetlights on the main road that took us to everywhere, so nighttime driving was not in the cards for me.

I had never held a housewarming party and was eagerly awaiting all the guests. Maggie was dressed perfectly as usual. She never missed the opportunity to show off her style. She was a very tall woman, with very long legs. I don't know if she ever wore anything twice in the whole time I knew her. I usually love a woman with such impeccable fashion sense and such a high self-confidence. She captivated my attention in those first few years.

On the Saturday of the housewarming, all the food was out, and everything looked festive! We all (Maggie, Anissa, Rex, and I) waited patiently for the guests to arrive. As we sat and waited, there was some commotion across the street from us. An ambulance arrived, followed by the coroner. Our neighbor's son had passed away. I had never met him. He had succumbed to his long battle with cancer, I soon learned. So sad.

I guess that was a foretelling of how this afternoon would go. I felt horrible for the neighbors but hadn't met the brother that died. A death is an extreme emotion that kind of took over our whole party. Our party of four, that is. Anissa, Maggie, Rex, and I just sat there waiting for hours. Every now and then, one of us would get up and nibble on something, but nothing was happening. Nothing.

No one came. Not a soul appeared. Maggie did not seem surprised at all. I could not believe it. It really was another red flag waving. I then realized no one had responded to the invitations I had sent. We just sat there chatting. For some reason every time I spoke with Maggie, the topic of her shortage of cash was always a topic. And so, we all sat there with finger foods displayed beautifully, and no one to eat it. And then, one guest arrived. I was just going to start wrapping up all the food and put it away.

Meanwhile, there we all sat, waiting for a crowd to arrive, which never came to fruition. No one except one guest came. She was Maggie's niece. They called her Tootie. She was lovely and brought a beautiful houseplant! What a huge, eye-opening disappointment! All the food made was taken across the street to the family who had lost their son. Rex was not bothered or even surprised that no one came. It was the weekend, and he wanted to drink.

I began wondering what in the world was going on. I sent out forty invitations and not one RSVP! Very strange!

Chapter 13

After the debauched housewarming party, I still had not met many of his family. I kept hearing about them. From the day we arrived one of his cousins, Jeffrey, was there non-stop. He was nice but seemed to have many legal problems. We spent that first year building a huge back deck, a front porch, and planting bushes. I tried very hard to make this trailer a home. We had to plant grass, and we also added a huge above ground pool. We were less than ten minutes from the beach too. I liked all these things.

After quite some time, Rex decided to go to work. He told me he needed a company vehicle and some equipment, and he could make lots of money. He needed to, because my inheritance was just about gone by this time. I complied, and into business we went. For a while, the business kept the bills paid, but not that long. I did all the accounting and paperwork.

Rex did not believe in saving for a rainy day. He loved to make good money and blow it, while showing off to everyone how much he had. Looking back, that is a perfect sign of how insecure a person is. When they are so worried about how others "see" them, they are very immature. Rex was immature, with no self-confidence at all. He put on a great charade, but his armor was cracking, little by little, day by day.

Employees were not a problem. He put Jeffrey to work, along with Lola Ann and her daughter Lila Ann, plus all her stripper friends! Yes, there were plenty of workers! Unskilled didn't matter to Rex, he needed strippers on the job, to make the workday and workplace a happy place to be. The problem was on Fridays, the whole work crew got paid, and a lot of times Rex wouldn't show back home for days. It was okay, though; I was getting used to that behavior.

We had landed a contract with an apartment complex, which lasted about a year. Lots of hurricane damage had occurred there. During that year, I thought our business would actually turn a profit. We did. Instead of investing back into the business, though, the money was blown constantly by Rex. It was very disheartening to me. When a year passed, the job ended. With no more contracts, Rex and Jeffrey did small jobs, but never like the apartments.

Eventually the work dried up. The hurricane seasons were always plentiful with contracts but once the season was over, the work stopped. And since Rex didn't believe in saving, we needed money. Why put money away when you can blow it all and impress all the young strippers? Everyone would get laid off, and Rex would do jobs on his own or with Jeffrey, if Jeffrey wasn't in jail.

Rex screwed up jobs on his own though. He would bid for the job, get paid up front, and not finish the job. People were calling and complaining. One elderly lady died waiting for him to re-hang her finished cabinetry. I was fed up and told him I wanted my name off the business. We closed it, and he decided he would go to school to be a truck driver. He wanted me to co-sign on that loan for truck driving school! Well, I said no. Unfortunately, his uncle Ned got stuck with that bill!

Chapter 14

Now one of Rex's family members who was a mainstay at our home always was his cousin Jeffrey. He lived with us for years. He did go to jail quite a few times, but he would return every time he was released. His sister Lola Ann too. Both were crackheads! Poor Jeffrey was the scapegoat for all the bad things that happened. He was the outcast of this family! He seemed to always be in the wrong place at the wrong time and not doing what he got blamed for. He always seemed to have a good attitude though, even with a dark cloud following him wherever he went.

Jeffrey was your normal-looking guy. He had blond hair and was average height and weight. He had a positive attitude for everything he had overcome thus far. He had a wife, but they had separated by the time we moved there. He was very often in jail, and most marriages in that predicament didn't last. His wife raised the daughter, so I never got to know her very well.

We listened to Led Zeppelin together, and he knew every word, as I did! He taught me a few recipes as he was a great cook. His all-around cheerful attitude was refreshing and genuine to me. He was always with Rex and would do whatever he wanted. On the few times that Rex would be gone, he and I got along splendidly.

Now his sister, Lola Ann, was a totally different specimen. Lola Ann has been there and done that! I mean that in every sense. She has used her body to get whatever she wanted. Everyone in this family has used her body too. It didn't take long for me to figure out that her and Rex had been co-mingling all their lives! I was totally disgusted!

She wasn't exactly beautiful! She was tall and very skinny, as most crackheads are. She would call Rex in the middle of the night because one of her scams had gone awry, and he would jump out of bed to go rescue her. I grew very tired of all this quickly, especially since I learned he was having sex with her! The whole family knew it too, but he always denied it. I was experiencing serious regrets just in the first year.

Rex had a way of calming my fears and reassuring me that all his friends telling me these things were just jealous. They didn't have what "we" had, and they wanted it! We were fine and had to stop worrying. That didn't work forever though. I grew tired and bitter! Felt like a fool! I was homesick for my friends and my normal life. I wanted to go home! How could I?

Meanwhile the pool out back was full of all the kids from the neighborhood, and suddenly, the whole trailer rocked, as if we just had an earthquake. What was going on? The dog was barking erratically. As I ran out the back door to check on the kids, I saw what the problem was immediately. The pool had collapsed. Children were all over the yard as they had been expelled when all the water emptied. There were two under our deck. The neighbor's yard was thoroughly flooded. What a mess. An expensive mess. An avoidable, horrible mess.

I was beginning to see Rex's flaws. The well that had to be capped off, because he didn't follow the rules; the pool that just busted wide open because he didn't level it correctly, or better yet have the professionals do it. Costly mistakes that I was paying. It was ridiculous! He was very immature. He could see I was growing tired of his childish ways.

Chapter 15

I guess Rex picked up on this and decided he would propose marriage to me. I was shocked! He had never married anyone, and he wanted to marry me. Well, I said yes! I figured he must love me because he had never married before! He knew he needed to keep me happy at that time. How naïve and stupid I was! That day we went to the courthouse and did it. Maggie was there when we got home, welcoming me to the family!

I have no idea why I would marry him. I guess I was shocked by it! I had hoped he would change and become a better partner. I was not in my right mind though. The man I loved was a cheater and was having sex with his cousin. Did I really believe he would change his ways for me? I did, but he didn't change one bit. The real Rex came out!

As I said, he was a master manipulator when it came to convincing me that he would change his ways and become a good husband. After all, he had never married anyone else! He truly must love me, right? The tears would flow and all would be well for a while. After years of reflection, I know now the man has no heart and is incapable of loving himself or anyone else. He was a perfect con man.

All the signs were there too. I just shoved the signs away! I could change him.! I was in total denial! Denial is a pathetic and very dismal place to be while you are raising three kids. It is not the environment they should be subjected to. I regret it to this day. While my childhood, I thought, had been boring and uneventful, and very much normal. Looking back on the normalcy and predictability of my childhood, I am grateful for the morals and lessons learned from coming from a stable home.

My children were soon subjected to chaos and constant bickering going on in our household. Many family members are staying (taking advantage) and always something going on. Most of these things involved illegal activities! Needless to say the honeymoon was over before it even began. I just cooked and cooked more for all the various visitors and tried my best to live a normal life.

I needed my own life! I grew very tired of just cooking and cleaning for this huge family that always seemed to be at my home. I got a gym membership and went back to college. I began to have my own life. I wanted very much to return to where I came from and wake up from this horrible nightmare I was living.

In the summer, kids were out of school. We all swam daily or went to the beach. Those were good times. One summer Rex's two teens from another woman came. They had lots of stories to tell about their lives. They thought Rex had changed and was really getting his life together. We always had a crowd.

We spent many days out back in our pool. It would be full of all the neighborhood kids as well. We loved swimming, and all the kids were so tanned. Loved it. The pool would be full of people and just, suddenly, collapse. Then a new pool liner had to be installed, and it took days to fill it. It would flood the neighbor's yard and ours.

Well, the pool collapsed one day and all the people in it were flowing all over. Wow. Now how would we swim? Well... the beach was right down the road! To the beach we went. We were lucky no one ever was hurt by the collapse of the pool. Every time it happened, it just reminded me of when I had an inheritance and had told Rex to have the professional installers do the job. What a tremendous waste of money and water.

Chapter 16

I thoroughly loved going to college and having my own time to myself. It was nice to meet normal people. I performed very well in college and received many awards while attending. Rex would not go to the dinners with me where the college gave these awards out. I am sure now; he didn't like me being out of the house and doing my own thing. After the first few semesters, what he enjoyed most was the financial aid I received.

He would be around when the money hit the bank. Then, off he would run, to go blow the money! I eventually got my own personal account, which only caused more animosity between us. The days of us having a normal marriage were no more. In fact, we never had a normal marriage, it was all a facade! I was beginning to know his modus operandi and I was fighting it constantly. It began taking a toll on me.

His teenagers didn't stay very long. All the people, coming and going, and constant chaos showed them that he still was the same dad they had known before. They called their mom and eventually returned home. He fought with the son quite frequently, so I guess it was for the best.

I knew he was not faithful to me, and it hurt. His mother Maggie told me that he was dying and that is why he treated me so badly.

She was still using that story! Unbelievable! He would run off for days and days with Lola Ann and Jeffrey and leave me stuck at home with three kids and no car. I was going insane! Maggie kept telling me I was going through the "change," and that was why I would be in a bad mood!

I lost respect for Maggie more and more, every time she would placate me, or make excuses for her grown son's behavior. For her to continue with "he's dying" excuse was annoying and quite deceitful. It kind of explains why and how he continued in his narcissistic ways. All his life, he was adored by his mother! She had six children, but to her, he was the exception! He was the "golden child!"

He was abusive both physically and emotionally. I think the emotional is the most devastating, though, because it lasts so much longer. Black eyes eventually heal, but emotional abuse stays forever. Being told you are fat and lazy and undeserving of love over and over, has dire consequences. I began to believe it! His mom would see me with a black eye, and she would tell me not to argue with him! These people were sadistic to me!

At this point, I knew he never loved me. He loved my inheritance. He loved my student loans. I also felt like such a loser. I am sure my father was rolling over in his grave. I wanted to leave but I couldn't. Everything, the land and this huge double-wide trailer, was all mine! My inheritance from my father bought it all! Now that we were married, he would take it all if I left. I was told over and over that if I ever left with his daughter, I would be killed. I believed all of that.

He loved humiliating me in front of large crowds, which normally was all his family! No one would say a word. To be criticized and ridiculed in front of a crowd was horrible. It breaks a person down. They knew him and had seen this their whole lives! He was the devil to me. Life was pure hell, especially during holidays.

Chapter 17

Holidays were hectic at our house! So much food had to be cooked! I was exhausted! My children had always gotten up early on Christmas morning, so excited to see what Santa brought them! Here, though, not! They had to sit there and wait to open their presents! I quickly learned that it didn't work well here. Grandma Maggie would arrive sometime after noon, and she expected all the food to be ready at that time! When I grew up, we opened presents first thing in the morning! This was horrible!

I learned after years of all the holiday cooking to start preparing days before. In order to have all the turkeys done by noon took some practicing. I grew up with bread stuffing in my family, but Jeffrey taught me how to cook the best cornbread stuffing! I made both. We would prepare huge pans of cornbread stuffing. I grew to love it too. I always made bread stuffing too. Whatever stuffing was left over, I would freeze and use it later. Normally, there wasn't much of anything left over. Not even a slice of turkey for a sandwich.

When Maggie arrived, all dressed up in a new festive outfit, carrying the eggnog, the children could finally open their presents! Maggie always said, "No presents for me, I just need cash!" Then off to make her eggnog concoction! She normally brought her brother Ned.

I truly loved Ned. He lived in my hometown, and I had met him before we moved. He was very unapologetically gay and proud of it! We got along splendidly. He ran a beauty salon in a big city and had many famous clients and stories to tell! We could talk for hours! Along with hair styling, he, too, was an artist! When I first met him, he had been working on a huge canvas that looked very similar to a Monet painting! Very talented man, he was.

Meanwhile my house was full of people from one end to the other, and Maggie was on her second eggnog! The radio was blaring "Cocaine," and Maggie was sashaying around as she sang the lyrics! Rex would join her, and they both would belt out the song! What a scene! I had never seen anything quite like that. Not the traditional holiday that I was accustomed to. Children of all ages were running through and grabbing finger foods and desserts.

Anissa would be there with Reginald, her sugar daddy. They always dropped in for a plate and usually would leave shortly after to visit more people. Lola Ann would be there with her latest catch. None of them lasted long with her. She always stopped by though for a quick bite before she would leave and head out to score some drugs.

She had a daughter, Lila Ann, who had followed in her mother's footsteps in every way; she would have been there too, if she wasn't in jail. She had one daughter at the time; Tiffany was her name. She and my daughter basically grew up together. Lila Ann, much like her mom, was a crackhead as well. She didn't eat much at all, and if and when she did, she didn't gain a pound. She was constantly being arrested for drugs and prostitution. When she was out of jail, the family was happy to see her.

The mood would be festive for a while and then as the evening grew near and guests would all trickle out, the nightmare would begin. Rex, as I said, would become enraged every holiday! I knew alcohol did that to him, but holidays did it too! Every holiday would start out wonderfully and end up horrible! What is it about holidays and physically abusive men?

All I know is my dad loved the holidays, and that is how I grew up. He loved singing Nat King Cole's "Chestnuts Roasting on an Open Fire" and trimming the tree. He would spray all our windows with the fake snow. I guess it reminded him of colder Christmas seasons up north. We (him and I) hung Christmas lights up outside our house. I have many good memories of Christmas from childhood that can never disappear. For a decade, though, they did. I soon learned that all the work of cooking and cleaning up and wrapping presents were fine, but the evilness of Rex and his temper would kill any holiday vibes. I dreaded holidays. So sad.

Chapter 18

Had I known then what I know now about narcissism, perhaps all the red flags waving at me in the beginning of this relationship might have prevented all the aftermath of pain and confusion I experienced. Life, though, is all about learning. With me, learning the hard way is how it's done. I can reflect on it now and understand it perfectly. Rex kept his narcissism well-hidden, though, until I had moved states away from my home. I was an easy target.

Narcissists must shower their spouses with unbridled love and affection. He was a master at that! I was in a very vulnerable position, going through a divorce, which made me a perfect target. I felt like a failure, and that was obviously very apparent. As I said before, I have never been one to jump right into another relationship that quick. I broke my own rule there. I batted all the red flags away as soon as they appeared!

After a narcissist has you, hook, line, and sinker, they are well on their way to destroying a few years or more of your life. The sad part is you are allowing them to. Meanwhile you are beginning to doubt yourself. The behaviors of jealousy and control that you found so endearing at the onset of the relationship, are now even worse. In fact, you are haunted by them. That attribute of anger and violence is constantly in the back of your mind, as tempestuous attacks become more frequent.

You, as the spouse of a narcissist, learn to walk on "eggshells" and live your life on the offensive, always. You try, unsuccessfully, to prevent frequent outbursts by carefully always manicuring a perfect scene. Anything that you can possibly do to avoid an angry outburst from them. The problem is, it's not you, it's them. Nothing you do is going to be good enough. You cannot avoid anything. They are like an angry, tired toddler, with a full diaper and wanting a bottle. You try, though, and are constantly reminded that you yourself are not in control, and can never be, with a narcissist.

It is the most demeaning, infuriating, and self-deprecating feeling to realize, if you do, that you cannot fix them. They will never, and didn't ever, love you. They only love themselves; however, I have my doubts about that. How can someone who loves themselves treat others with such loathing and non-empathetic decorum? I have never been one to give up. I will try and try and try again, to fix imperfections in my life. With a narcissist, you must relinquish and let go! Much easier said than done.

As tenacious as I am, I just hated to see something I could not fix. I have always been able to fix whatever maladies I encountered in my life thus far, so why couldn't I fix him? It would mean that none of this whole situation was indeed brought about by fate. That was my illusion of how this whole relationship began; I just simply refused to accept the reality. I was in serious denial.

Chapter 19

I was quite busy with raising my kids, cooking for crowds, and cleaning up after crowds and of course going to college full time. I learned that the more responsibilities I was given, I adapted and was able to accomplish anything that I set my mind on. Of course, at the time, I didn't know that. The one thing I couldn't do was make Rex love me. I am not a quitter, though; never have been. I worked hard to keep him happy and working, so the bills would get paid, and there hopefully would be less violent outbursts.

What I couldn't prevent was the violence and cruelty he continued to show me. I learned when he wanted something, his whole attitude changed. It was clear as day! He would come home and be considerate and helpful, but I soon learned and feared when he did that; it would end up terribly because I had learned to say "NO!"

He could not stand the word "no." He would scream and break things and intimidate, but a black eye or a fat lip didn't scare me anymore. I knew it was temporary. When he would hurt me badly, with visible injuries, all of us had to stay at home. Kids could not go to school; we were all prisoners in our home. He always ripped the phone from the wall so no calls to the police could be made.

I still believed that everything was my fault. If I had just cooked the perfect dinner or baked that cake. If I could just lose weight, he would appreciate everything and love me. Your mind plays cruel tricks on you when you are in an abusive relationship. If you hear it enough, you believe it. I desperately wanted to leave with my three children and our dog but wasn't brave enough to. I wasn't going anywhere without all of them. I stayed. I refused to accept defeat.

As I was cooking one evening, the kids and the whole neighborhood were swimming, trapsing in and out of my house with their wet feet. I heard a loud noise, and the trailer shook. It was the pool collapsing, yet again. Just another reminder of what a dismal world this hillbilly hell was.

I just began escaping. I began drinking heavily. It was how I made myself feel something. It masked my pain, and I continued with all that had to be done. I was. A well-functioning full-fledged alcoholic. I know now that alcohol only masks your pain and, in the morning, when you wake up with a horrible hangover, your pain and regrets have returned two-fold. And yet…you do it again. What a horrible, vicious cycle to live in.

I learned that narcissists don't like to be reminded of their failures. I never spoke of the pool again. It would not be erected again. I was done with the whole sadness of it all. The one thing that brought us all happiness was down and we were all upset about it. It was plain stupidity.

Chapter 20

Now I told you Rex had a huge family. That is an understatement! Maggie had six. Where were they? Well, her two eldest were Clayton and Didi. The next two were Dan and Kayla. Rex and Anissa were the last two. I learned through all of them that once her husband died, the two oldest males were given to an uncle to be raised. Lucky them. By the time I met them, they both were successful and had wives and children. And they both owned homes; not houses on bricks or trailers. It seemed to me that distancing themselves from this family was good for them!

Clayton was a boilermaker and quite successful. He had white hair when I met him and vivid blue eyes. Dan had red hair and owned and ran a shrimp boat. He worked very hard and was successful as well. Didi was a teenager when her father died. She decided at that age, as she saw her whole family splitting up, that she would get married and move away. She too seemed to benefit from the distance. She had dark hair like Clayton had in his younger years.

Kayla was the other sister. She had lived in my hometown. She had been married for twenty-seven years to Jefe. Kayla had reddish-brown hair and reminded me of a female Rex, if there was such a thing. One day after work, her husband asked her if she needed anything from the store. She told him what she wanted, only he never returned. She was devastated! She ended up moving in with Anissa, right next door to me.

I liked Kayla; we had some fun times! When she moved to our town her two sons followed. One of them, the oldest, was Enrique, and he had a wife, Lovey. She was a dancer. They had three young girls. Also, his younger brother Rolando came. He was single at the time. They were constantly near us, either at Kayla's with their mom or at our house hanging with Rex. This family grew bigger and bigger every day.

Now that was all the children of Maggie. When her husband died, she sent the two oldest boys to an uncle's to be raised. Didi left home and married and moved to the opposite side of the country. The other three, Rex, Anissa, and Kayla, were all put in a home. Meanwhile, Maggie married four more times. Not sure how or when she went back and got them. She did, though.

I know all six of them looked different. Some had dark hair. Some had red hair. None of them even looked related. Rex stood out because of his dark skin. He had a permanent dark tan that none of the others had. Maggie knows the truth and that is her story to tell. I know she absolutely worshipped Rex! He was the "golden child!"

Now I know mothers are not supposed to have favorites, but Maggie showed so much favoritism to Rex that it called for more clarification from me. I never confronted her about it, but I sure wondered. It was always in the back of my mind. The other siblings didn't seem to care. My inquisitive mind was on it though. I finally just began believing that Rex had a different father.

Guilt can do funny things, though. I am not saying she was guilty of anything, but her actions toward him were indisputably different to how she treated the other five. One day she came over and informed us that she was paying for his burial expenses. Why? Who knows? Did she know something I didn't know? Was he truly dying of cancer like she had said all along? What about the other kids? Why was she only paying for his? It made no sense to me. This woman, every time you saw her, complained that she was broke all the time, yet she is now paying for his burial, on top of all the other things she couldn't afford. He was working, too, and could afford to pay his own burial expense, while the others weren't.

Chapter 21

Rex had been driving a big rig for a while, and all three of my children were in school now. Life was somewhat normal. I was finishing up my school and earning a bachelor's degree. Maggie and Ned had bought the house on the other side of us. I was surrounded by family! As I said, I loved Uncle Ned, so I was very happy he lived next door. We would sit outside every day and shoot the shit while waiting for the various school buses to drop off all my kids.

Anissa and Maggie had traveled across the country to help Didi. Her husband of over twenty years was dying of cancer. It was a nice time. Then I got a call from Rex saying he got fired in Atlanta and he couldn't bring the truck back. This was the first time that he had gotten fired while out on the big rig. He never thought rules applied to him. Off to Atlanta I drove.

When you drive a big rig for a major company, they have a GPS tracker that tells them where you are always. Rex never followed rules, and he was fired twice for doing God knows what. Each time I had to go retrieve him from wherever he got fired from. Why do some people think they can just continue to keep bucking the system? Stupidity? Immaturity at its finest! Or an overly adoring mother, who blamed her son's bad behavior on everything else except what it was, a serious lack of morals.

It really irked me. Eventually, he had to find a company or a truck owner that he could drive for with no GPS. He behaved like a child, and I was beyond fed up with him. His check would go to the bank on Friday, and I would tell him what bills were due. Many times, since he had started driving, the bills were not paid. He would tell me on Thursday what checks to write, and I would. ALL THE CHECKS WOULD BOUNCE! One time he was in Mexico having a grand time! It was beyond infuriating!

Well, after Anissa and Maggie had been at Didi's helping her with the death of her husband, they called with devastating news. After they buried her husband, Didi was diagnosed too with cancer. Stage five. She didn't have much time. A huge hurricane was coming, and Didi wanted to come home to die, with all her family.

Chapter 22

Now, I told you there were many hurricanes in this area, and it just so happened that when Didi's airplane landed, a major hurricane hit. All the power was out, and it was a very balmy and hot day. We put her in our bedroom, with a generator powering a window unit to keep her as comfortable as possible. We needed to secure hospice for her. I guess the most important thing, though, was that she was safe and cool during the onset of her stay. Normally, when the lights were out in that area post-hurricane, it would take many days to restore, but this time we only had to wait two days. God was there!

Once the electricity was restored, we set her up in our den. I spent many hours getting to know her. She was still eating, and she even got out of bed and came out on our back deck once! She was a very normal and hard-working lady. She worked at Walmart for eighteen years! That is hard work! She had accepted her upcoming death and had no regrets. The hospice was wonderful too. In my opinion, those hospice nurses are God's angels preparing the way to heaven.

That one time she got up was the only time. Within a week she was hardly eating and bedridden. She still talked but not as much, and soon she would sleep more than anything else. I had never been around death. My family had died in hospitals, not in my house. This concept of dying with all your family around was very strange to me. My children were all there too, with Anissa and Maggie. More would come as time passed and death was near.

Before she had become non-cognizant, Rex set up a bank account for her. He told her he could handle all her affairs since she couldn't. The money for all the funeral arrangements would go into that account. He was so thoughtful in that way. She slept for the last few weeks. Family would come and go to pay their respects.

I remember the morning she died. Anissa came and woke me and told me. I called Rex, who had just left with the truck, and he returned immediately. The kids were still asleep and had to go to school that day. I got the kids up and fed and out the door to the bus without telling them. They had seen her sleeping for weeks and they never knew she had passed. Once the children were gone, the mayhem began.

The whole family gathered around her body, at her bedside. They all spoke their last words to her. I watched silently from afar, then we all prayed. Each one of them had said a few touching words and cried. It was very poetic. I remember thinking how touching and nice it was for this to be happening at home instead of in a hospital. It felt so personal and real. I was waiting to hear what Rex would contribute to the salutations. He was gone though. Where was Rex?

Chapter 23

There would be no prayers or sweet, touching words from Rex. He was gone! Where was he? He had scooted out the door when it all began. Turns out, he had hit the nearest liquor store. When Rex returned with a bottle of Crown, I knew what kind of day this was going to be. Meanwhile I began cooking many breakfast casseroles and trying to make sure there was plenty of coffee for all.

Everyone was so solemn and relieved at the same time. Poor Didi, she had to deal with her husband of twenty something years becoming sick and ultimately dying and then immediately after, her own untimely death. How harsh of a reality is that? Mortality is something all of us must face. We all hope that when our time comes, we will lie down one evening, after telling our loved ones we love them, and that death will occur peacefully and with no burden to our loved ones.

Whether you believe in fate and destiny, or you believe that death occurs half-hazardously because of some mistake we may have made, the ultimate truth is, we are all going to die. No mistaking it. If, and when, we don't know. This, Didi's death, was the first one I have participated in. Making her final days happy, comfortable, and at peace was an honor for me. I will never forget it, nor do I want to. I can only hope I can die with dignity as she did.

As we waited for the coroner's office to arrive, the talk quickly changed to money and services for Didi. Anissa and Maggie were positive they would receive a large chunk of her estate. After all, they had been at her home helping with the dying husband for all those months. My mom always said, "Don't ever bet on a come." Besides that, don't you help your family members without expecting a payday? I would like to believe that. They would soon learn otherwise.

Rex had overseen that account. She had to be buried, but there was no longer enough money for that. Everyone was arguing suddenly. Where did the money go? Only Rex knew, and he was getting drunk and combative at this point. I was still cooking breakfast for the crowd. It was insanity at its finest, as poor Didi lay just steps away dead. I could just imagine her, on her way to heaven, and looking back sadly on this family of hers.

Rex hadn't expected her to die so soon. Although hospice was only two days off the estimated demise. I was astonished how they knew. I guess if you're in the business of dying, you probably ought to know. In the end, Reginald, Anissa's sugar daddy, would pay, hoping to be paid back one day. She had to be buried, though. And where was the coroner's office? It had been several hours. Well, nothing happens expeditiously in Hillbilly Hell.

Chapter 24

I served the food and had to get out of the house. All the bickering and screaming while Didi lay there lifeless was getting to me. The poetic symbology of dying at home with your loved ones was replaced by the reality of family misery and screaming and bickering just inside of my home. It was sad. Many decided to go at this point, seeing that the money for her burial was short. Why hang around? Might be expected to pitch in.

As I sat there on my front porch, listening, a florist pulled up and delivered a beautiful house plant in memory of Didi. Ah… some sunlight in this somewhat dreary existence. I had phoned my mother earlier; she had sent a plant. Normalcy was restored for just a minute. I continued to sit and just enjoy the "awayness" of it all, hoping that the neighbors couldn't hear.

Eventually I meandered back inside. I began cleaning all the dishes and trying to decide what was for lunch. At last, and finally, the coroner showed up. They took Didi away, to prepare her for her final resting place. There was a calmness after. A finality of sorts. I began the grieving process. I sat and contemplated life and death.

What it must feel like to be dying. I imagine it is sad but peaceful. Everyone says, "I just want to lie down and go to sleep and never wake up." Imagine, though, if that was the case; no one would ever go to bed angry or sad. This world would be a totally different place. There would be no more regrets or guilt because we would resolve all our indifferences before going to sleep. How nice that seemed at that moment. The screaming from inside my home brought me back to reality.

All in all, I was honored and appreciative of having got to honor Didi's last wishes. Everyone was on their best behavior while she was alive. I really admired the hospice team! They were wonderful! It takes someone very special to be so positive and uplifting to their patients, knowing they are all dying.

I have decided, when it's my time to go, I want to use hospice. Much better than some hospitals and different nurses every few hours.

Chapter 25

It turns out, Didi left nothing to her family. She left everything to her best friend. Poetic justice, I guess you could say. This was a real blow to the family; they had already begun spending it. Anissa had bought Kayla a new set of dentures. The sad part was that she was convinced the dentures did not fit properly. She kept gagging with them.

One night when Kayla was over, drinking with Rex, he told her he could fix them quickly. He proceeded to file them down with an electrical tool he had. As quickly as she received the teeth, they were gone, ruined by an electric file. I guess you can figure out how that turned out. To this day, Kayla still has no teeth!

Everyone in Rex's family had false teeth. Rex told me that they all had inherited gum disease. Lila Ann was out of jail on her birthday. She was at our house as another resident. It was her twenty-first birthday! She received her dentures that day. She had just had her second baby and would sleep all day while that poor baby cried. She acted like she couldn't hear him crying. I would wake her to take care of him.

I remember the night she arrived. She arrived very pregnant and ready to burst. She wanted to have that baby! Maggie told her if she drank some castor oil it would speed up the delivery. Anissa and I were off to find castor oil and a milkshake to mix with it. Within three hours Anissa had taken her to the hospital; she was indeed in labor! Who knew? Well, I did! With my second son, I had him naturally. My midwife had told me to try it. It worked for me! It took longer to drink that disgusting shake than it took to give birth. My ex-husband had come off the road for the birth and was leaving in two days, and we tried. It was disgusting though.

Lila Ann, like her mother Lola Ann, had drug abuse problems. She was constantly being arrested for solicitation of herself or drugs. She learned from her mother and her father. Her father and mother were no longer together, and he overdosed and died in the bathroom while visiting his mother. That is the sad succession of that family.

Lila Ann knew many young girls and always had them at our house. More fodder for Rex. I was more than fed up with this at that point and starting to really pay attention to my instincts by this time. I came home early from school one day and found Rex home from work, and Lila Ann up and about, instead of sleeping. They were both sitting on couches and out of breath. I guess I surprised them! I knew he was sleeping with her then. I wanted to throw up!

When confronted about it, Rex replied, "Don't be stupid. I used to change her diapers!" Not only the cousin, but the cousin's daughter! Nothing at all could shock me anymore! The insane mess I was living in was literally disgusting to me, and there was no escape in view. I acted more and more like a robot. Just cook and clean and show no emotion about anything. It was best that way. No one in this whole backwoods state was remorseful or ashamed of their ludicrous behavior. Cousins sleeping together; nieces too.

Now that doesn't mean his violent outbursts stopped! It meant I was not going to participate anymore. I refused to care or show one iota of emotion! He could throw his fits, shout out angry epithets, and toss me around, I just refused to respond. I am not sure if this helped anything, but it helped me! I needed to survive, and that is how I did.

Chapter 26

One Sunday, the children and I were home all weekend. Rex had never come home from work on Friday. We were stuck at home with a dwindling food supply and no car and no money. I was getting more and more upset by the minute. Rex shows up and goes straight to bed. I told him I needed money for the grocery store. He handed me the card, and off I went to shop.

I spent more time than usual because it felt so good to be out of the house. I spent more than my sixty-dollar allowance too. Rex would be passed out when I got home, and I was going to take advantage of the situation. He was too exhausted from partying all weekend. He would not want a fight. He just wanted to rest.

As I began loading the groceries in the car, I noticed something very alarming. My favorite leather jacket was not in the car. Where could it be? I figured I had taken it out and hung it up at home. I apparently just didn't remember doing it. The groceries were loaded, and I began the drive home.

As I approached the house, I noticed a sheriff's car near our house. As I got closer there were three sheriff's cars. Hmmm. What could be going on? As I pulled in the driveway, I could see they were just parked there, not necessarily at our house, though. I began taking the groceries in, and a friend of Rex's was there. He told me Rex took off out the back door and into the forest of trees behind our house. Rex asked him to watch the kids until I returned.

First of all, the police weren't there for our house. At least I didn't think they were. I did notice they were gone now. Rex didn't return until much later that night. He sure had a guilty conscience. Or perhaps he had done something while he was away for the weekend. Who knows? Never did find out what all that was about.

At that point, I remembered that my leather jacket was missing. I looked everywhere but never found it. Jeffrey had driven our car earlier that week, and I soon learned that my leather jacket paid for crack. I was beyond upset. I was so done with this place.

Chapter 27

As the years passed, I began to wonder if I would ever have a normal life again. Apparently, this place I was living in was not my home. I felt as if I lived to please everyone who lived in my home. I had no problem with my kids, but the revolving door of sinister characters was always around, and the never-ending job of feeding them all was exhausting. My whole life was exhausting. I felt as if I had thrown all my morals and beliefs out the window, to just "fit in" there. I wasn't that person. I didn't fit in there. This was not my home.

I became depressed. All the aches and pains I had had been due to depression. I knew I had to get out of there, but I didn't know how. The thought plagued me day in and day out. I would get calls from old friends from my hometown, that friends of ours had died. Life was going on and off all over, but not here. I did not, could not attend their funerals. It was sad.

I hadn't even spoken to Lulu in years. Last I heard, she wasn't doing so great. All my old friends I eventually lost contact with except for Facebook, which was wonderful. I missed them all but could watch their lives evolving every day because of this great invention.

Nothing changed there. I was in a loveless marriage, and he was gone most of the time. His family surrounded me but never loved me.

There was no love there. That was the problem with this place. No one had morals here; no one. At first, I thought parents who party with their children were cool. The problem was, the kids were not being raised properly. It was a sad, tragic place to live. I began to despise hillbilly hell.

My mom called one day and invited Rex and I to go to Chicago for my cousin's wedding. I was ecstatic! Yes! Rex, however, wanted no part of my family. That was okay with me. I was going to Chicago, and it would be wonderful. Anissa agreed to watch the kids while I went. I was so excited. I needed a coat, though, and my leather jacket was gone. That was okay, I would take Rex's leather jacket. It was a little big but worked fine.

Weddings in Chicago are big events compared to weddings in the South. It was a beautiful wedding, and I got to see all my cousins and family, and they were all normal! I saw people I hadn't seen since I was a teenager. As a child, we always took annual trips there, and it was just like I remembered. It just reminded me of how there are normal people out there, and they lived in homes (not trailers or houses propped up on bricks) and had wonderful lives.

After the reception, which went on for hours, my cousins, my mom, and I all retired to our hotel rooms. My mom was tired. My cousin knocked on the door and asked if I wanted to join them at the bar downstairs, and I said, "Of course!" We all continued to drink until the wee hours of the morning, just as the Irish do! I drank so much; I ended up leaving Rex's leather jacket behind. I lost it. Never got it back either.

The next morning, I was sleeping in and dealing with a hangover and the phone rang in my hotel room. It was my oldest son. He called to tell me that while I was gone, Rex had a big party. He said Rex told them he was leaving and moving out. He did too. He also took my big-screen TV that was built into a wall, out of the wall. It left a huge, gaping hole from my back den into my bedroom. Wow. What a way to ruin the rest of my trip.

When I returned home, he was gone. The hole in the wall was just a reminder. How sick and twisted was that? He had moved out and in with his nephew. Not sure what that was all about, because within one week, he was calling and saying he wanted to come back home. At that point, it didn't matter if he was living in my home or at his nephew Rolando's home, we were no longer together. I worked and was in grad school and was busy. Didn't really care what he did; except when he was there, mischief lurked.

He didn't fix the huge, gaping hole in the den that looked straight through to my bedroom, but I didn't figure he wasn't staying long, and I just didn't care anymore. At this point the home was beginning to need upkeep and maintenance, and he just ignored all of it. He didn't care. I didn't either. We both lived our lives separately but at the same address.

Chapter 28

After all the years there, I became immune to shock. Nothing surprised me anymore. I was a raging alcoholic, and that was how I dealt with all the putridness of this dismal hell. I was like a robot. Get up, cook for all who were current residents at my house. I didn't believe I would ever find a way out of there, so I adapted.

Rex was on the truck most of the time, and when he was gone, Anissa would babysit when I had to go to school. I remember vividly walking out of my room one morning to go and Anissa said, "Look! Airplanes just crashed into a building in New York!" I froze in place! Yes, it was September 11th! I told her it had to be Osama Bin Laden! When the second plane hit, and the newscasters were speculating, she was shocked I knew!

They did not watch the news there, none of them. Unless it interrupted their cable show! They all said the news was depressing! Wow. I just didn't belong there and kept wondering why I was. No wonder this place was like ten years in the past! No one wanted to better themselves or learn anything new. How depressing it was.

Rex was on the truck and blowing money wherever and with whoever he wanted. That was fine with me. My home was filled with teenage kids from the whole neighborhood. All these kids grew up with mine and I loved them all. My cookie jar was always full, and they were always welcome! Probably it was the best of times there.

Rex would come home on the weekends, and the house would be full, but then he would be gone again. It worked out perfectly. Kayla, whom I had grown close to, lived next door in Anissa's house. Her son, the oldest, Enrique and his wife Lovey did too, along with their three daughters. I spent many afternoons and evenings hanging with all of them.

Bonfires and cold beer and music. No Rex around to ruin the festivity. Her three kids hung out with my three and it was somewhat perfect. At that time Kayla was drinking. She was such fun to hang out with! Looking back, those were the best times I ever had there. That part of his family was the best to me. They knew Rex was a jerk and treated me horribly, but they didn't treat me badly. They were nice too when Rex was around.

As I said before, Rex loved to humiliate me in front of crowds. Most of his family would not do anything but look away. That hurts so badly and does wonders for your self-esteem. Enrique and his family treated me kindly though, and it felt good having someone in this horrible place that I could be myself with and have a great time with. Finally, though, they found a house and moved. Their first house was around the corner, and I would still visit them.

At that time, Enrique was a stay-at-home dad. His wife was a dancer. She worked nights and got paid in tips. Sometimes she got inebriated and lost all her tips. It couldn't have gone on forever, and it didn't. One morning on her way home from work, the car she was riding in was hit badly. They had to use the "jaws of life" to extricate her from the car. She was then transported to a hospital. It didn't look like she would make it. In fact, her body was tagged as if she was dead on arrival.

Those doctors brought her back though. It was a miracle. She, then, after over fifty different surgeries and years of rehabilitation began to live a normal life again. Meanwhile, Enrique began working and supporting his family. I have always believed God stepped in and made that choice for them. He gave them a second chance. There would be no more dancing for Lovey. Eventually they moved again, this time further, and I would see them during family gatherings but not on a daily basis anymore. I missed them but still saw them, so it wasn't that bad. Kayla was still next door, and we hung out almost daily.

I truly believe God stepped in at that moment in their lives and brought about change, only the way He can do. They had three young daughters that needed more guidance in their upbringing. Now the mother, Lovey, would be at home daily, and they could perhaps have a more stable life. None of those children had started school yet, and two of them were past due.

Enrique began a job and made good money. Meanwhile, Lovey was in rehabilitation for her numerous surgeries and to learn to walk again. It was a horrible ordeal, and thankfully the family survived it. God has a way of teaching us those hard lessons. We sometimes do not even realize there is a lesson to be learned until it is years later. We look back and realize that He saved our lives.

Chapter 29

One of the weekends he was home, he told me he wanted to take in one of his sons from a previous relationship. The state was involved, and someone needed to take him. This boy was one month younger than my oldest. He was a teenager. That would be tricky trying to feed so many on the sixty-dollar food allowance I had. I told him that our marriage wasn't a real marriage, and I would be the one having to do everything, but he insisted. I had learned everything Rex did benefitted him only, so why did he want to take this boy? I figured the state would investigate Rex's background and not even allow it.

I was wrong. This state, which was so backwoods and shady, allowed him to come. Of course, he came, and I got him registered in school. I grew to love him as my own. He soon witnessed the violence and stupidity that we all did, living with an abuser. His name was Jonas. I would like to think he enjoyed living with us, when Rex was not there. The social worker who interviewed Rex remarked, "Papa was a rolling stone!" This was after she found out he had five kids out there, but only took care of one. Mine. How backwards this state was.

He did come from a troubled past, but he was, for the most part, a good boy. He needed a good environment to live in. He truly was Rex's son because he was the spitting image of him. He reminded me of Rex as a child. The Rex I had a crush on, so many years ago. He told me, though, that he never felt like Rex's family accepted him. I told him not to worry about that. None of them accepted me either.

He now was the oldest of my teenagers! I had three boys. Three hungry boys, and was supposed to feed our whole family on sixty dollars a week. It was very disheartening! Each week I would drive to various stores, trying my hardest to make sixty dollars stretch. I would go to the bread store and buy discounted bread. I would also hit the various grocery stores, looking to grab discounted meat. It didn't work though. Rex would have a "meltdown" every time I confronted him about it. God kept us alive then! That is the only explanation I have for those days. We grew close, and one day the school called and told me he had been injured at recess. I had to pick him up, and yes, he was injured. He had a broken leg. I took him to the hospital, and we both sat, waiting patiently for him to get a cast. Hospitals, especially emergency rooms, can take many hours, once they have stabilized you, so we just sat there and talked. We got along well. He never disrespected me. He was a good boy.

Next thing I know, the nurse is telling me I have a call! Rex called the hospital saying we needed to get home. What was the holdup? I told him Jonas had a broken leg, and we were waiting on the orthopedic surgeon to get a cast. He screamed, "WELL, HURRY IT UP. THE KIDS ARE ALL HOME FROM SCHOOL AND SOMEONE NEEDS TO COOK DINNER!" Really? I am pretty sure Maggie came from next door and cooked. Thanks, Maggie.

We didn't get home till late that night. Poor Jonas. Thank God our insurance covered this mishap. He stayed home a couple days with me and then he returned to school. He couldn't take the bus, so I drove all the kids. They all liked that better. Not me so much. There were three schools, elementary, junior high, and high school. Lots of lines to sit in. We do what we must, though, and I always brought a good book to read while waiting.

Chapter 30

My mom had called months before and had booked a resort for our whole family to go to Disney World. None of us had ever been. We were all excited. Now, though, we had Jonas with a cast. He still wanted to go, though, so we took him. The one who kept making up excuses and trying to back out was Rex. Our relationship was horrible, and in hindsight I wished I had let him. We didn't spend that much time together, and when we did, it wasn't pretty.

Disney World was a dream! We stayed at one of their many resorts. Luxury had no limits! It was dreamy. All our food was included, and they had many different themed resorts, each with a different type of food. One would have barbecue and steaks, while another would have Mexican or Italian. Those Disney people think of everything!

What drove me crazy was the crowds of people, everywhere, at all times! We went in early October, but I don't think they have non-peak times. It is totally packed 365 days a year. I do not like being crammed into a theme park, with a million other people and just trying to get around. I very much enjoyed just relaxing poolside at our resort though.

When you have a rocky and volatile relationship with someone, do not pack three teenaged boys along with their sister in a van to go on a family vacation! While Disney World is and was beautiful, especially staying at a resort, where all meals were included, I knew for sure this was the last place that I would ever go with Rex. He was in a vile mood the whole time and it constantly spilled over onto everyone else. It was scary. I could feel a major change coming. I just didn't know what would change.

I am forever grateful that my mom did this, but I am personally traumatized every time I think of that trip. I remember one of the days, he was carrying the camcorder around and he set it down. He forgot to retrieve it when we got up again. Later, he realized he didn't have it. He had all of us backtracking all over and cussing us out and terrifying all of us! The teenagers and I were all crying. The place was packed full of tourists watching us. Finally, I suggested we check lost and found. There it was!

That was our last night there, and after all of that he said we were going back early to go to bed. We didn't get to see the last part or ride anything else. The kids were all so let down. So was I. How could I think he could behave any differently at Disney World? It was the end of everything. I was so disappointed in myself for letting him go. And I hated myself for how I let him hurt my kids.

It wasn't exactly the end. He had one more encore.

Chapter 31

When we returned home, he had been saying he needed to borrow some money to buy himself a vehicle. That was the best thousand dollars I ever spent. I knew if I did it, he was going to leave me. This was the change I kept feeling. I went with him and put the money down on a Jeep. He wanted me to put it in my name. He had burned my name and credit to the ground by this time though. It was put in his name.

We all had been around the corner at his nephew's house, and he was having fights with everyone. We eventually left and returned home. He was in a mood for sure. He decided he wanted to leave and asked where his keys were. No one knew. He had been driving! He went from one end of the house, slamming stuff and breaking everything on the way! All the kids were scared and crying. I was a wreck as well. I was so tired of this same scene of intimidation and viciousness.

I was afraid but looked for the keys frantically. I wanted him to go. I had been feeling this change coming. Here it was. Where were the damn keys? Your instincts kick in at times like this. I wanted those keys, but my inner voice was saying to get out! Where would we go, though? No car and four kids and I had grown very tired of going to the neighbors. They were more tired of it than I was. I had to end all this madness.

He made one mistake. While he was on the other side of the house, I picked up the phone, dialed 911, and hung it up. When he returned, the phone rang. At this point, all the children and I were making our way out the front door. Normally all phones were smashed; not this time. Once he realized the police were coming, he shoved us all aside and took off running down the middle of the street. He grabbed my laptop that I had purchased for school too. The sight of him running down that dark street with my laptop was a sobering relief. I knew it was finally over.

All the times he had unleashed his fury and rage and madness and cruelty on all of us were finally over. I was still in shock. It was such a relief. It is hard to explain how I felt. His Jeep was still there, so I knew he would return. We had time to get away, though, and we were safe. All four kids were terrified and still crying at how abruptly this all happened in a matter of minutes.

I knew it! I could feel a change coming for weeks. Would this be the end? No more battles, bruises, or black eyes. He just took off running down the middle of the dark street. I had finally learned to act on my instincts quickly, instead of being afraid and thinking of doing it, but cowering instead. The adrenaline was rushing at this time. For once in this entire decade, I felt that "all was well with the world." All the pain and madness that led up to this moment seemed to leave me right then. I didn't care if I ever saw him again. I had to make sure we could get out of there, in order for him to leave.

The kids and I were so relieved he was gone. They ran next door to Grandma Maggie's house, banging on her door and crying. She answered and told us all to quiet down because Ned was sleeping. Never mind that her son, the "golden child," had just put us through hell, ranting, breaking, smashing everything. We just needed to all be quiet. I was done! He had left me plenty of times and always came back. Not this time.

We had to go back, but he was gone. I still did not feel safe there. The police came and took us to a safe place. I hated leaving my dog, but we fed him and left extra. We were gone and safe and that was all that mattered. In a few days, Anissa would call me and tell me that he had found the keys, and he was gone. It was safe to come back home. That was the best day that I had had in the last decade. We were free!

We did return but none of us wanted to stay there anymore. The boys slept with bats under their beds, determined to defend our home if need be. My daughter slept with me for many years. I would let her go to her friends to stay the night, but she always came back home. She feared her father would hurt or kill me. We continued living like that for the next year. Every day, we were ready, should he return, but he wasn't. He didn't call. He was gone for over a year. My children were starting to come out of their shells and live a somewhat normal life.

I was sad, angry, scared, and just couldn't understand why I would mourn him leaving, but I did. It was a big change, and changes can be scary. I grew emotionally and started to feel normal again. It took years to fully recover. Perhaps this place wasn't as bad as I thought. With him and all his family ignoring me it was quite a relief. No... I wanted real normalcy. I wanted to go home.

We all got along great and were doing very well without him. His family was spying on all our activities and reporting back to him. His mom kept telling me, "Don't file for divorce, make him do it!" Right? Did she really believe I would trust her or any advice she would give me? No. I got a legal aid lawyer, and she was great! The best part of that was she was free. I got a job and then two and even a third. I was supporting these kids, and they were growing up, and there was a closeness to all of us that had been missing before. There was a harmonic balance that is hard to explain.

The problem was, Jonas was still living with us. I loved him, but the social worker told me he would have to leave eventually. He was not my son, he was Rex's. I had inquired about adopting him, but she told me that he wasn't a "blood" relative, that wouldn't happen. I was sad. The day finally came, and he was moved out of my home.

I would eventually put the home up for sale. His leaving was the best part of this whole story. Selling a used double-wide is impossible though. It wasn't going to happen. They are overpriced to begin with, and a used one is just not going to sell. I would have to take that loss.

Chapter 32

He left me and went straight back to the girl who had been my best friend for years. They had been together for months. Yes, Lulu and Rex were an item now. Maggie came over and very coldly told me, right in front of his daughter and all the kids, that his daughter was not his daughter, his son Jonas could go back into state custody. He was done, and I needed to be too. His whole family, except Uncle Ned and a few others, ex-communicated themselves from me after ten long years.

It was the coldness of how Maggie said that to me, in front of all my children, that really sticks with me. I had learned, though, how she was. That was the least of my worries. She never liked me, and the feeling was mutual. I saw a lot of Rex in her. Both were wicked to me. I didn't really feel sad yet. It was a new beginning.

I figured out where he was when the bank statements came. That day I was shocked! I knew enough to know that Lulu and he wouldn't last. If they did, good for them. I didn't care! The man was, and could never be, happy. The pain of a friend doing that to me hurt more than any loss of him. Only the people that know you so well, with all your flaws, misgivings, and fears, could hurt you to the core. I let that happen. It would be almost twenty years before I would ever love again.

At that moment, though, all the pains I used to feel daily, which came from stress I am sure, were gone. I felt free, lighter than air. I had a beautiful credit score when I moved there; it was ruined. I had now four kids to raise; the thought of sending Jonas into state custody never crossed my mind. I had a new degree from college. I would get a job, actually three, and work hard, and we would survive. We did too.

I worked two full-time jobs and one part-time, and we survived. The teenagers, my three, helped a lot. They would make sure everyone got up and got onto the school bus. The times I felt sad were those first holidays. Maggie would walk straight across my lawn to go to Anissa's on the other side, carrying holiday dishes and her eggnog. The street in front of my house would have cars everywhere! I finally snapped at Maggie and told her to stop walking through my yard. She complained that she was having problems walking that far. I guess that was supposed to make me pity her. It didn't.

I noticed, though, later, she would throw the walker to the side and sprint whenever she heard Rex's big truck pulling up. She had those long legs, and when she wanted something, she could really move. She was a hypochondriac, and all her sicknesses were in her mind. She, just like Rex, was so transparent to me. When they wanted something they both coerced with conniving ways. She would act sick, and he would act nice. They were experts!

It was pathetic. However, we were all living stress free. It was beyond "poetic justice."

Chapter 33

About a year later, Rex returned to divorce me. He brought Lulu, and they lived right next door in an old trailer. As I washed dishes and looked out my kitchen window, I could see them. I had a front-row seat to their little love nest! After our divorce, paternity tests revealed that my daughter was in fact his daughter; he had to pay child support. Turns out, he didn't. Who cares? I didn't. Maggie did come over and say she was happy that our daughter was indeed her grandchild. I was beyond done, though, with all of them. So much pain and stress Rex and his family had caused me.

The only one that was happy about Rex reappearing was my daughter. That was her father and she loved him. Never mind that he had been gone for over a year and never called once; he was back now. He really spoiled her a lot at that time, and it caused a lot of static with her brothers. We lived through it though.

Now he and Lulu lived right next door. All the chaos was next door and not in my house anymore. It was wonderful. We got great amusement watching all the chaos next door. It was funny. The constant screaming, slamming, and utter stupidness was not in our home anymore. Living in a backwoods state was taxing on me. I was ready to get back to recycling and city water and laws that were relevant, up-to-date, and followed.

When I first found out that Lulu and Rex were an item, it felt sickening. I had spent many years with her and her family. I felt a part of that family. I couldn't believe that they were all right with this. They knew Rex and I were married. It hurt me to the core. I was utterly devastated. After some time, I realized that he did not tell them the truth. The truth was horrible. Narcissists never tell the truth. They must make themselves look good.

At least I convinced myself of this, and that is how I dealt with the pain. Lulu had become an alcoholic too after her divorce. From what I had heard, she wasn't doing so well. She was living on her parents' property. I hadn't seen her in years. She did call, though, every once and awhile. She didn't call to tell me she was now with my husband though.

We didn't even speak for years after this. I felt betrayed by her, and I knew she was going to get exactly what she deserved. A narcissist is not picky, and they treat all their victims the same. He treated her the same way. Twice she was sent back home on a bus, brandishing a black eye or two. She kept coming back for more though.

One afternoon it was cloudy outside, and it looked like it was going to rain. All the kids and I were watching a movie. The phone rang and I answered. It was Anissa, and she was screaming at me. She said my son had shot a bee-bee gun at Lulu. I said, "When?"

She said, "Just now and we have called the police." I told her repeatedly that we don't have a gun of any sort and we are watching a movie. She hung up!

About thirty minutes later a sheriff was at my door. He took my son next door and I followed. He had him sit in the back of his patrol car. I joined him in the back of the police car. Lulu was in the doorway of Anissa's house, pointing at my son. I told the cop, "We have been in the house watching a movie. She is lying." He soon figured out that Rex and I were going through a divorce. He then told Rex to take this up in court. He believed us!

Meanwhile I was furious, to say the least, with Lulu. Rex, too. I felt like he was trying to hurt my son. This did not sit well with me.

Meanwhile, the sheriff let us go home. My son had never been in any trouble, and to sit in the back of a police car and be accused of such a thing was killing me! Divorces can get ugly but leave my kids out of it!

If I hated my life before, it would get more and more disgusting by the day! If I was at the grocery store, Lulu would be there. When I did dishes at night, there she was, next door, partying with what used to be my family. It was like living in a bizarro world. You had to laugh about it eventually. What I didn't realize at the time was that Rex was out of my life now. All the terror and anger we had to live through was gone. It was next door but not in my home! I had three jobs, and my children were all good. Life was improving, I just hadn't realized it yet though.

When you can feel compassion for someone who has hurt you so badly, you are healing. You may not know it, I sure didn't, but it was happening. Life couldn't have been better at this time. That year he had been gone did wonders for all of us. I began to plan our escape from this horrible hell we had lived in. First thing I did was move from that trailer. I did not want any part of that life anymore. The constant daily sightings of Rex and Maggie, not to mention Lulu, was too much for me. I had enough stupidity for a lifetime.

I contacted a real estate agent and put the land and the trailer up for sale. Most importantly, I got the hell out of Hillbilly Hell and never looked back. Later we found out who the culprit was. It was another kid from the neighborhood. No one liked Rex in that area. They all knew what a violent, stupid man he was. That day, though, I prayed that Lulu would get everything and more of what she was dishing out. Rex used her, just like he used me! She still hadn't realized it yet though.

I rented a home in a different neighborhood. A nice neighborhood, with regular homes that were not hoisted up on bricks. When spring hit, the whole yard bloomed with hydrangeas, tulips, and all kinds of beautiful foliage. It was gorgeous. Whoever had lived there before had planted a beautiful landscape. It was like heaven on earth to me.

I was divorced now and everything I needed to do was done here. I contacted my mom, and we began to plan our return home. Within a year, we moved. A decade of my life was spent there, and many lessons were learned. I met a few that I keep in touch with on Facebook, but most importantly I no longer regard that decade as a waste of time. I grew up and learned some very painful lessons. All the aches and pains were gone, and I was beginning another decade. A decade of healing and peace and learning to love again.

All the abuse and sadness my children and I incurred in Hillbilly Hell we finally moved. We went back to my hometown. We have never looked back and don't want to. I took a huge loss on that trailer, but I am sure my father, in his grave, is okay with that. We are all alive and well and happy.